STEPHEN J. SLADE

Adlai Stevenson

Adlai
Stevenson

by LILLIAN ROSS

J. B. LIPPINCOTT COMPANY

Philadelphia and New York

1966

O NE of the big ifs in recent history is what our country might have become and how the world at large might have been affected if Adlai Ewing Stevenson had been elected President of the United States thirteen years ago. Early in 1965, talking about this if and about the various blows Mr. Stevenson had had to take, I asked one of his closest friends, Mrs. Edison Dick, who had known him for forty years, whether she felt sorry for him. "Not at all," she said. "I can feel sorry for a person who hasn't prevailed against fate, but I think he has prevailed." Last year, I saw quite a bit of Mr. Stevenson, with the intention of writing about him in the pages of *The New Yorker,* and the more I saw of him, the surer I felt that she was right. Of course, every time I listened to him speak, and every time I read his prose, I regretted that he wasn't doing some writing in those pages himself. "I had a taste for literature and for the academic," he said to me about a year ago, early on a Sunday morning —a corner of time he had reserved in his backbreaking schedule for one of our talks—and he went on, "It's been part of the luggage I've carried in public life which doesn't yield public dividends." As always when he talked about

himself, there was a lightness in the texture of his voice, and now its tone conveyed a detached, wry enjoyment of his own plight.

That morning was two days after his sixty-fifth birthday, and he had been awakened at his apartment in the Waldorf Towers—his official residence as United States Ambassador to the United Nations—at one in the morning by a caller from the State Department who wanted to tell him about the country's first major air strike in Vietnam. When I arrived, around eight o'clock, I learned that Mr. Stevenson had been on the telephone with government officials intermittently throughout the rest of the night. Nevertheless, he looked fresh and alert, and he was newly shaven and pink-cheeked, dressed in pin-striped navy trousers, a brown tweed jacket, a blue shirt open at the neck, and well-worn bedroom slippers. He had a new crisis on his hands, he said. Also, he was wondering what to do about a number of house guests—friends who had come from far points to help him celebrate his birthday. They would be getting up soon, and meanwhile he had arranged for several meetings, on the crisis, to be held later that morning at his office at the United States Mission to the United Nations. He expected to attend a hastily called meeting of the Security Council in the afternoon or evening. Notwithstanding this program, Mr. Stevenson showed no inclination to call off our talk. At the time, I was preoccupied with the broad question of what *might* have been, for him, and, as a result of having already spent a good many hours watching him and listening to him, with

ADLAI STEVENSON

the further question of what might still *be*. I asked him,
after one jangling telephone call, what he would like above
all else to be doing at that moment. "I'd like to be out on
my farm, in Libertyville, pruning trees," he said, and then,
with that delightful, friendly Stevenson laugh, he added,
"And I'd like an opportunity to get some rest. I've had
about eleven days' vacation all told since I went into this
job, four years ago. I'd like to do some reflecting and
reading. I have an enormous accumulation of books I'd
like to read. I'd like to be able to spend some time with my
children and my grandchildren. And I'd like to travel, in a
leisurely way, when I wouldn't be on exhibition and
wouldn't have to perform. In the past twenty-four years—
ever since I went to Washington during the war—I haven't
had an opportunity to travel without having the travel
coupled with ceremonies or the writing of articles or the
taking of notes. But my first responsibility is to the
President and to this job. I'd like to be useful as long as I
can be. I've been so involved with affairs of my own
generation I'd feel a little bereft if I were *not* involved. It's
tempting sometimes to dream about a tranquil old age, but
I think I'd be a little restive."

In those four and a half years, in addition to attending
sessions of President Kennedy's Cabinet, and then of
President Johnson's, and attending meetings of the
Security Council and the General Assembly and endless
United Nations commissions, Mr. Stevenson had several
speaking engagements a week, usually at luncheons or at

dinners. (When he was not attending breakfasts, luncheons, cocktail parties, dinners, cookouts, and suppers given by other people, at least half of which were connected in one way or another with the United Nations, he usually played host at two or three of them a week himself.) One of his extracurricular appearances in August, 1964, shortly before the Democratic Convention, was at the final dinner of the annual meeting of the American Bar Association, held in the Grand Ballroom of the Waldorf-Astoria, where he was to make a speech. I met Mr. Stevenson at his apartment a few minutes before he was due at the dinner, and accompanied him to the Grand Ballroom, marvelling as we went at his fantastic energy. He appeared to be wholly absorbed in what he was about to do; there was no sign that he had walked into hundreds of other ballrooms set up for two or three thousand chicken dinners to be eaten by uncomfortably dinner-jacketed or strenuously gowned goers and doers—lawyers, engineers, actors, opera lovers, zoologists, and all the others. From the Bar Association dais, he looked into thousands of unanimated faces without mirroring anything of what he saw; his expression remained lively. An audience of lawyers, Mr. Stevenson had warned me, was by nature extremely conservative, and it seemed to me that he was relishing the challenge. The usual string orchestra, in red-and-gold uniforms, played "Some Enchanted Evening" from a balcony, and Mr. Stevenson, looking up, gave the musicians a nod. He remarked to one of the lawyers on the dais that a pre-dinner highball might be a good idea, and the lawyer

offered him what he described as his own "slightly used bourbon." Mr. Stevenson smiled gratefully and took it. Then, as his custom was at dinners of this kind, he put on his horn-rimmed glasses and started studying the speech he had written and making improvements in it. As usual, there were interruptions for autographs, for the introduction of wives, and for announcements from citizens that they had voted for him in 1952 and/or 1956— information that was frequently offered in a near-recriminatory key, because, in a success-happy age, he had not won.

In addressing the A.B.A., Mr. Stevenson tried to make his gray, largely humorless audience laugh, and he succeeded. "I've been paying dues to the A.B.A. for forty years," he began, before starting to read his prepared speech. "Now I have the privilege of making a speech. Without compensation, of course. [Laughter] There's something about a Presidential election year that makes even retired politicians restless. [Laughter] At the United Nations, I sometimes yearn for the peace and tranquillity of a political campaign. Everybody wants to talk to me about politics, evidently forgetting that I am now a statesman. [Laughter]" With his audience warmed up and at least somewhat relaxed, Mr. Stevenson said what he had come to say. The pronouncements of Barry Goldwater were much in the minds of Americans that August, and Mr. Stevenson made it clear that he, too, was thinking about them. "I have thought that the strength of the American political system lay precisely in its lack of extreme

contrasts, in its rejection of dogma, in the fact that rigid ideology really has no relevance to our great political parties," he said. "And this system has remained intact for more than a century—the most stable, durable, and adaptable system the world has ever seen. But now, as society and the world become more complex, some people want to repeal the whole thing. They seem to yearn for the old simplicity, for the shorthand analysis, for the black-and-white choice, for the cheap-and-easy answer, for the child's guide to good and evil. The very color and diversity of our pluralistic society seem to confuse them; they want it plain and unitary." The lawyers sat there. Quite evidently, they were not on fire. But Mr. Stevenson wound up with undiminished passion and undiminished devotion to what he wanted to tell them. "The greatness of the issues calls out for greatness in ourselves, to vindicate democracy, to speak for freedom, and to make our profoundest affirmation of faith in the American way of life," he concluded. The applause was dutiful. However, Mr. Stevenson didn't seem disappointed as the thousands of lawyers began to plod out of the ballroom. One of them, a chubby man, rather pale and ill at ease, came over to Mr. Stevenson and, after telling him that he had voted for him in 1952 and again in 1956, said, "I remember 1960 in Los Angeles. That was quite a demonstration they put on for you." "They raise more hell when I'm *not* a candidate than when I am," Mr. Stevenson said, with his laugh.

Later on, in reply to a question, Mr. Stevenson told me that he thought he could speak fairly easily now, although

it had taken him many years to reach that point. "I had a terrible time as a young man," he explained. "I was very self-conscious, and I could never speak in public without getting paralyzed with fright." He said that his eldest son, Adlai E. Stevenson III, who is a lawyer and a member of the Illinois House of Representatives, was developing into a good speaker. "He's a very thoughtful student of public life," Mr. Stevenson said. "He has a natural dignity about him, yet he has a wonderful sense of humor. I don't know whether he's got the stomach for the crudities of politics. I don't think he'd ever be any good as a demagogue."

At the Democratic Convention, a week or so afterward, Mr. Stevenson, who was a delegate from Illinois, seemed to enjoy himself. He particularly enjoyed the fact that with him in Atlantic City were his three sons—John Fell and Borden in addition to Adlai III—and John's wife, Natalie, and Adlai III's wife, Nancy, both of whom were delegates, the former from California and the latter from Illinois. Mr. Stevenson joked with the boys about the Convention activities of the two young women, who, he said, had a natural talent for politics. "Natalie is so damn important I want to follow her around and pick up crumbs of wisdom," he said. Later he told me, "I've been going to Conventions since 1948, and this is the first time that I've been able to get to the *Convention*. Heretofore, I've always been locked up in an icebox. When you're being nominated, you can never get out of your hotel room. You eat sandwiches. You walk from microphone to microphone.

You put your head out the door and look up and down the hall. Then you settle in to write a speech, and furtive characters peer in at you from time to time. And out of all this comes imperishable American political prose."

In Atlantic City, Mr. Stevenson was again besieged by people who wanted to tell him that they had voted for him. Hotel doormen, addressing him as "Adlai," told him that he should be the Presidential nominee, and Mr. Stevenson courteously thanked them. A woman came over to him and said, "You have such a nice warm face," and Mr. Stevenson courteously thanked *her*. A couple of women, both wearing plaid Bermuda shorts, told him that their names were Rhoda and Sally, that they taught second grade somewhere out West, and that he was their "favorite candidate." "We ought to go back to school," Mr. Stevenson said gallantly. "Things have improved."

In the course of some Convention high jinks, Mr. Stevenson said to me, "They used to call me aloof. Actually, I love to be with people. I *enjoy* them. But you can't have things both ways, and when you have to work on a speech, you can't be shut up in your room working and out with people at the same time. However, I've never been able to go for the smash-and-grab kind of person in politics, and, for some reason, that made a certain number of people say I wasn't being practical. It's entirely possible, I think, to be a responsible and completely effective public official without being a smasher-grabber."

One question I'd wondered about for some time was how the legend had arisen about Mr. Stevenson's being

"indecisive," and I asked for his explanation of it. "It arose largely from one fact, and that was that when President Truman asked me to be the Presidential candidate in April of 1952, I declined," he said. "I declined for two reasons. One, I was already an avowed candidate for reëlection as Governor of Illinois. I didn't see, in justice to the people of Illinois, how I could be a candidate for two offices at the same time. And, two, I didn't *want* to run for President. I had no such ambition. I wanted to finish the job I'd started in Illinois. For the ensuing six months, I was beset right and left by individuals and delegations from all over the United States putting pressure on me to announce that I was a candidate and to enter the primaries and compete for the nomination. When I refused to do so and never wavered and was very decisive, and then was subsequently nominated at the Convention and accepted, I was told, 'You're indecisive.' Nobody can believe you when you say you're not a candidate. It's a curious thing. The more decisive you are in not seeking an exalted office, the more they say you're indecisive. My very decisiveness was attributed to what they call indecision. Sometimes you look back at it all and it seems almost comic. I don't have any feeling of bitterness. Both times I ran, it was obviously hopeless. To run as a Democrat in 1952 was hopeless, let alone run against the No. 1 War Hero. Even so, if it hadn't been for that going-to-Korea business, I might have beaten him." There was no sound of regret or vanity in Mr. Stevenson's voice; he spoke with as much enthusiasm for the subject, and as much appreciation of its inherent

interest, as if he had been discussing some episode in history that he just happened to know something about.

The talk turned to Washington, D.C., and I asked Mr. Stevenson whether he liked the place.

"I've lived so much of my life there and know it so well it's difficult not to like it," he said. "Washington was different in the thirties, when I first went there. My feelings are bound up with the way it used to feel during the long evenings—sitting in the gardens of those Georgetown houses in the hot summers, perspiring, with our visions and with our dreams. When I was there during the war, we didn't have much time for fun, but the work itself was fun. In those days, we were interested in ideas. Now it's all so much personality talk, gossip, and rumor— who's up and who's down. The criticism is sort of brittle now, and there's a lot of malice and mischief."

On the first day in Atlantic City, a television interviewer asked Mr. Stevenson, "Governor, how do you feel about the Convention? Are you *sad?*" (He was always addressed as Governor, even though his last title was Ambassador.)

Mr. Stevenson looked far from sad, and he told the television interviewer that he wasn't sad. "I'm hoping to see all the many old friends who fought and bled for me in hopeless causes," he said.

In the raucous, emblazoned Convention Hall, he was presented on the stage in the customary man-who fashion ("the man who was twice given the nomination for President by his party"), and the audience received him with a boisterous ovation. It was Mr. Stevenson's mission in

Atlantic City to deliver a tribute to Eleanor Roosevelt.
Again, he had worked hard, and had come up with a
memorable piece of writing to present as a speech.
"Thank you, my friends, for your welcome—and for
all your loyalty and comfort to me in years past when our
party's fortunes were not as bright as they are tonight" was
his beginning. He continued, "For what I have done and
sought to do for our country and our party, I have been
repaid a thousandfold by the kindness of my fellow-citizens—
and by none more than you, the leaders of the
Democratic Party." The audience now seemed politely
patient. "It is of another noble American that I am
commissioned to speak to you tonight," Mr. Stevenson
said, projecting his intimate words into the echoing
vastness of the Hall. "She has passed beyond these voices,
but our memory and her meaning have not—Eleanor
Roosevelt. She was a lady—a lady for all seasons. And, like
her husband, she left 'a name to shine on the entablatures
of truth forever.' There is, I believe, a legend in the
Talmud which tells us that in any period of man's history
the heavens themselves are held in place by the virtue, love,
and shining integrity of twelve just men. They are
completely unaware of this function. They go about their
daily work, their humble chores—doctors, teachers,
workers, farmers (never, alas, lawyers, so I understand);
just ordinary, devoted citizens—and meanwhile the rooftree
of creation is supported by them alone. There are times
when nations or movements or great political parties are
similarly sustained in their purposes and being by the

pervasive, unconscious influence of a few great men and
women. Can we doubt that Eleanor Roosevelt had in some
measure the keeping of the Party's conscience in her special
care?" It seemed, at that moment in Convention Hall, that
almost nobody wanted to think about the question he had
just asked or the answer to it; now that the nominations
were in, the audience's mind was on who else was going to
get what. The delegates adjusted their paper campaign
hats and shifted in their seats, and many of them looked
as though they were now having some difficulty tolerating
their former candidate. Nevertheless, he went the course
with what he had come to say: "She thought of herself as
an ugly duckling, but she walked in beauty in the ghettos
of the world, bringing with her the reminder of her
beloved St. Francis, 'It is in the giving that we receive.'
And wherever she walked beauty was forever there." The
delegates gave Mr. Stevenson's speech a nice hand, and the
name of Eleanor Roosevelt was not mentioned at the
Convention again.

About a month later, on September 22nd, it was Illinois
Day at the World's Fair, and who but Adlai Ewing
Stevenson, of Illinois, was tapped for the Day. "I've been
promising Bob Moses I'd come, and I'm glad I finally
made it," Mr. Stevenson said as I joined him in one of
those Greyhound motorized chairs. He looked expectant,
and gave a Stevenson smile. "Illinois Day presented me
with a day off from the war in Cyprus," he added, with
satisfaction. It was about ten o'clock in the morning, a time

that is very popular for ceremonies, and Mr. Stevenson was
one of the first of the invited guests to arrive at the
Illinois Pavilion for the Day. Among those who turned up
later were Benny Goodman, Cab Calloway, Governor Otto
Kerner, and Robert Lincoln Beckwith, a great-grandson of
Abraham Lincoln and one of the sixteenth President's
three surviving direct descendants. A press agent handed
out a release stating that none of the descendants have
children and that "it is expected the Lincoln blood will
discontinue with them." Mr. Stevenson read the release
with what seemed to be respectful interest. He looked with
pride at the sayings of Lincoln's inscribed on the outside of
the Pavilion, among them "WHILE MAN EXISTS IT IS HIS DUTY
TO IMPROVE NOT ONLY HIS OWN CONDITION BUT TO ASSIST IN
AMELIORATING MANKIND." Then he was ushered into the
darkened theatre of the Pavilion, where about three
hundred devotees of Illinois were assembled and where the
sensational attraction was the six-foot-four-inch mechanical
figure of Lincoln, which was to sit, stand, and speak
Lincoln's speeches. But first Mr. Stevenson had the
privilege of sitting through an hour-and-a-quarter Illinois
Day program that included the dedication of a memorial
to the late Illinois Secretary of State Charles F. Carpentier;
a kind of pageant about the history of the State of Illinois;
some folk songs by students at the Old Town School of
Folk Music, in Chicago; a short speech by Mr. Beckwith; a
somewhat longer speech by Governor Kerner; and the
bestowal of prizes on winners of the Chicagoland Music
Festival. Then Mr. Stevenson was introduced. He was brief

in his remarks. He said, "Governor Kerner, Mr. Beckwith, Mr. Moses, distinguished guests, sons and daughters of Illinois: We meet here in the midst of the American quadrennial political Olympics, at a time when the air is both figuratively and literally filled with the spoken word. Any man of conscience and sensitivity should exercise particular care in anything he says in public (or, for that matter, anywhere). I am conscious of the remarks of Illinois's greatest son, Mr. Beckwith's great-grandfather, and an intimate friend of my own great-grandfather Jesse W. Fell, of Bloomington. In his message to the Congress in December, 1862, he addressed himself to political leaders of his own and future generations. In the midst of a bitter fratricidal struggle, where tempers and factionalism colored the judgments of many men, Lincoln warned, 'If there ever should be a time for mere catch arguments, that time surely is not now. In times like the present, no man should utter anything for which he would not willingly be responsible through time and in eternity.'" The devotees of Illinois looked blank. The words of Lincoln as Mr. Stevenson spoke them did not appear to make much of an impression. The audience was evidently waiting for the mechanical Lincoln to speak. This Lincoln—a Walt Disney creation, manufactured at a cost, the Illinois press agent told me, of ninety thousand dollars—followed Mr. Stevenson, and its speech was billed as "Great Moments with Mr. Lincoln." Mr. Stevenson listened to it in apparent fascination. The mechanical Lincoln really did sit, stand up, and make a speech—by means of a recording by an actor—in a very deep, melancholy, Lincolnesque voice. I thought the robot was creepy, but Mr. Stevenson admired it. "It's a marvel," he said. "In one speech, the quotes put together ran all the way from 1838 to 1864."

At the United Nations one afternoon in January, 1965, I waited at the entrance to the General Assembly Building for Mr. Stevenson, who was scheduled to deliver a major address before the Plenary Session in General Debate. "The U.N. is finished," the uniformed guard at the entrance where I stood stated to me in a highly certain tone. He was an American, and he knew what he was talking about. "Next year it won't be here," he went on. "Look at the faces of the delegates, especially the Africans. They don't want the U.N. in America. Look at the Ambassador from Hungary. Ice-cold. He doesn't talk to nobody. We're through here. Red China wants to start its own U.N. Who wants this one?"

The session was called to order by the chairman, His Excellency Mr. Alex Quaison-Sackey, of Ghana, at three-thirty. The gallery was packed. With Mr. Quaison-Sackey on the dais sat U Thant. The United States delegation sat with delegates from Upper Volta on its right, delegates from Belgium and Austria behind it, delegates from Thailand and Syria in front of it, and delegates from the United Republic of Tanzania on its left. Mr. Stevenson—his glasses on, the plastic earphone for translations over one ear, a lumpy briefcase open on the floor at his side   sat putting a few more touches on his

speech. Then he seemed to listen intently as the first
speaker, the distinguished representative of Mali, talked for
quite a while, in French, about being "non-aligned but not
for imperialist aggression." There was perfunctory applause.
A young man introduced as the Foreign Minister of
Morocco made a halting address, also in French, on what
I gathered was his interest in peace. There was no
applause. Then the Foreign Minister of Pakistan took the
floor to discuss, in English, the "crude, absurd, and
mischievous" remarks of the distinguished representative
of India dealing with what he charged was a fraud that
had been perpetrated by India upon the five million
people of Kashmir. "They are the ones whose right to
self-determination has been denied," he said. "They have
the right to be free. Justice must be done!" There was
perfunctory applause. The next speaker was the distinguished
representative of Afghanistan, who said in a speech in
English, which took thirty-five minutes, that Afghanistan
was following a policy of friendship with her neighboring
African nations; that the United Nations was the only
place of hope for saving the world from destruction; that
the United Nations' financial crisis, with other crises, was
deepening anxiety; but that the Afghanistan delegation
was not getting discouraged. There was mild applause. Mr.
Stevenson didn't seem to be missing a word. I was sitting on
the sidelines, behind some observers who kept calling out
friendly remarks in Portuguese to the delegation from
Brazil, which was seated nearby. I assumed that the
observers were also from Brazil. The noisiest observer was a

middle-aged lady who had several rings on her fingers; one ring was set with a pearl the size of a lima bean, which was surrounded by a big cluster of diamonds. She held a mink coat in her lap, and stroked it nervously, without letup. She didn't close her mouth for more than two minutes at a time throughout the address delivered by the distinguished representative of Afghanistan. A number of the delegates looked asleep, or half asleep. Mr. Stevenson glanced occasionally at the text of his speech. Otherwise, he was wholly attentive. At 4:59 P.M., he was called. "The last speaker is the distinguished representative of the United States," the chairman said.

Mr. Stevenson started by saying that it was his first opportunity to extend congratulations to the chairman for the way he had conducted that session of the General Assembly. Then he said, "I have asked to speak at this late date so I can share with all delegations, in a spirit of openness, my government's views on the state of affairs at these United Nations as our annual general debate comes to its conclusion. Certain things which I shall say here today have to do with law, with procedures, with technical and administrative matters. So I want to emphasize in advance that these are but manifestations of much deeper concerns about peace and world order, about the welfare of human society and the prospects of our peoples for rewarding lives."

The group of Brazilians in front of me, including the noisy bejewelled lady, were quiet for the first time. They were paying attention. Everybody in the hall seemed to be

awake and listening. What Mr. Stevenson was talking about was the U.N.'s financial crisis, which was mainly the result of more than a hundred and thirty million dollars in overdue assessments owed by Russia, by eight other Communists nations, and by France, Belgium, Paraguay, South Africa, and Yemen. Under Article 19 of the U.N. Charter, any nation that is two years in arrears automatically loses its vote in the General Assembly. It was one of Mr. Stevenson's chores to express the opinion of our government (which happens to carry the largest part of the United Nations' expenses) that there should be no voting in the General Assembly until Russia paid at least one-third of its overdue assessments. And so Mr. Stevenson, in his speech, was going to warn the General Assembly against the notion of a "double standard" of assessments for United Nations peace-keeping operations. "We cannot have two rules for paying assessments for the expenses of the organization—one rule for most of the members, and another rule for a few," he said. But before he reached that point in his speech he made some remarks about the United Nations as a whole. "I speak to you as one who participated in the formulation of the Charter of this organization, in both the Preparatory Commission, in London, and the Charter Conference, in San Francisco," he said. "I recall vividly the fears and hopes which filled and inspired us as a second world war ended—fears and hopes which brought us together in an attempt to insure that such a world catastrophe would never again occur. At those conferences we labored long and diligently, we tried

39

to take into account the interest of all states, we attempted
to subordinate narrow national interests to the broad
common good. This time we would create something better
than static conference machinery—something solid enough
to withstand the winds of controversy blowing outside and
inside its halls. This time we would create workable
machinery for keeping the peace and for settling disputes
by non-violent means—and endow it with a capacity to
act."

The speech had about five thousand words, which he
had checked for policy with the State Department, as he
always did in his job, but which he had put together
himself, in his own remarkable way. It took him about
forty-five minutes to deliver. He wound up saying, "I, for
one, cannot escape the deep sense that the peoples of the
world are looking over our shoulder—waiting to see
whether we can overcome our present problem and take up
with fresh vigor and renewed resolution the great
unfinished business of peace—which President Johnson
has called 'the assignment of the century.'" The hall was
full of delegates who were supposedly divided, but the
applause for Mr. Stevenson was immediate and strong.

For most men, delivering a five-thousand-word speech
might constitute a week's, or even a month's, work. For
Mr. Stevenson, it was a small and routine part of a
twenty-four-hour schedule. The very next morning, he was
speaking in the General Assembly again—this time paying
tribute to Sir Winston Churchill, who had died three days

earlier. Afterward, he conferred with his associates, and then went to a meeting with U Thant, and on to a luncheon for twenty-four people being given by Liu Chieh, the Chinese Ambassador to the U.N. From the luncheon he rushed back to his office to meet with a couple of congressmen from Florida who were en route to Churchill's funeral, and then to confer with Norway's Ambassador to the U.N., who had some ideas about a compromise plan for the countries owing assessments. After that, the new Ambassador from Malta to the U.N. paid a courtesy call on Mr. Stevenson, and for half an hour Mr. Stevenson listened intently to a discussion of the people of Malta (there are three hundred thousand of them), and of the fact that during the sixteenth century, when Malta fell under the rule of the Knights of Malta, no Maltese were members of the knighthood, and of the possibility of setting up a Malta office in Washington. Having also seen eight other callers, Mr. Stevenson went off to a cocktail reception being given by the American-Arab Association, and after half an hour there he made for a party launching an Indian exhibit at the Union Carbide Building, where he found a mob of celebrated public figures, looking freshly bathed, rested, and barbered, and dressed to the teeth in formal clothes. Mr. Stevenson was wearing the same pin-striped blue suit, by now wrinkled and limp, that he had started the day in at 7 A.M. Vice-President Humphrey was at the party, tall and ruddy-faced and glowing, and was reminiscing about the Inaugural festivities, which had taken place a week earlier.

To Adlai

It's comforting to how

Lyn

There was a lot of kidding about the big hand Mr.
Stevenson had got when he arrived at the Inaugural
Ball. Everyone had flocked around *him*. "I never get
anywhere, but I get all the applause," Mr. Stevenson said,
making Vice-President Humphrey and several other guests
laugh. He looked at the exhibit for about an hour, and then
made for his apartment at the Waldorf. He had to change
to black tie and attend the Diamond Ball for the benefit of
the Institute of International Education, in the Grand
Ballroom of the Plaza Hotel. His housekeeper, Mrs. Viola
Reardy, told him she couldn't find his formal silk shirt and
shoes. Mr. Stevenson worried about the possibility of having
lost these articles, which were new. "You probably left
them at the Inauguration," Mrs. Reardy told him, and
Mr. Stevenson put on a regular shirt with his dinner jacket
and wore his daytime shoes.

At eight o'clock the next morning, Mr. Stevenson was on
a shuttle plane to Washington, where, at the request of the
British Ambassador, he was to give the memorial address
at the National Cathedral service for Sir Winston
Churchill. When he had found time to write the tribute
was something I couldn't figure out. It ran to about thirteen
hundred words. "Sir Winston Churchill is dead," Mr.
Stevenson said at the Cathedral. "The voice that led
nations, raised armies, inspired victories, and blew fresh
courage into the hearts of men is silenced. We shall hear no
longer the remembered eloquence and wit, the old courage
and defiance, the robust serenity of indomitable faith. Our
world is thus poorer, our political dialogue is diminished,

46

and the sources of public inspiration run more thinly for all of us. There is a lonesome place against the sky. So we are right to mourn." For Sir Winston Churchill the love of freedom was "not an abstract thing but a deep conviction that the uniqueness of man demands a society that gives his capacities full scope," Mr. Stevenson continued. "It was, if you like, an aristocratic sense of the fullness and value of life. But he was a profound democrat, and the cornerstone of his political faith, inherited from a beloved father, was the simple maxim 'Trust the people.' " Near the close of his tribute Mr. Stevenson had a sentence describing Churchill: "The great aristocrat, the beloved leader, the profound historian, the gifted painter, the superb politician, the lord of language, the orator, the wit— yes, and the dedicated bricklayer—behind all of them was the man of simple faith, steadfast in defeat, generous in victory, resigned in age, trusting in a loving providence, and committing his achievements and his triumphs to a higher power."

From the Cathedral, Mr. Stevenson went to the British Embassy for lunch and a reception. Then he went to the State Department for conferences on half a dozen pressing problems of foreign relations. He caught the three-o'clock shuttle plane back to New York, and at four-thirty, in his U.S. Mission office, he started a series of meetings with members of his staff. At six, he attended a cocktail party given for U.N. delegates from the African nations, in the U.S. Mission building, by the Harlem Lawyers Association and Ambassador Franklin F. Williams, the U.S.

representative on the U.N. Economic and Social Council. There an editor of the *Amsterdam News* named James Hicks told Mr. Stevenson he'd had trouble getting an advance copy of his speech about Churchill, and added that, come to think of it, during his Presidential campaigns it had always been difficult to get copies of his speeches in advance. "I'm afraid I sit up scribbling until the last minute," Mr. Stevenson told him. "Churchill was always rewriting his speeches until he had to give them." And then he had one of those characteristic funny afterthoughts that constantly bubbled up in him: "But that's where my similarity to Churchill ends."

Mr. Stevenson was due at eight-thirty that evening, in dinner clothes, at a concert of the New York Philharmonic, but when he was about to go home to dress, his secretary sent word to him that a group of educators working for UNESCO were gathered in the Savoy Hilton apartment of his old friend William Benton, the former Senator from Connecticut, who was now the U.S. representative to UNESCO, and that Senator Benton had been stricken suddenly with pneumonia and had to go to the hospital, so there was nobody to speak to the group of people in his apartment. The educators from UNESCO wanted to hear all about the history of the U.N. situation in reference to Article 19, and the problems arising from it. In a manner in which there appeared to me to be no hesitation, no doubt, no resentment, no self-pity, Mr. Stevenson immediately headed for Senator Benton's apartment. Ambassador Marietta Tree, the U.S. representative to the U.N.

Trusteeship Council, who was present at the cocktail party, rode up in the car with him; she was on her way to a dinner being given by the Pakistani Ambassador to the U.N., she said.

"I went *last* week," Mr. Stevenson told her playfully. "You'll be offered a hookah. I smoked a hookah last week. Watch your step with that hookah, my girl. Ambassador de Beus, of the Netherlands, smoked the hookah with me last week and then told me, 'My public vice is women. My private vice is the hookah.'"

Mrs. Tree said that she would watch her step.

"And don't eat too much," Mr. Stevenson said. "The food is delicious, but you'll find that nothing is green or ever has been."

"Long time no see!" the Savoy Hilton doorman called out to Mr. Stevenson as he got out of the car.

On the sidewalk, Mr. Stevenson almost collided with a jaunty young man carrying a briefcase. The young man halted and gave Mr. Stevenson an admiring little bow. "My pleasure!" the young man said, yielding the right of way to Mr. Stevenson.

"Why, thank you," Mr. Stevenson said, graciously bowing back.

He had less than an hour in which to go home, dress, and keep his date for the Philharmonic, but he walked into Senator Benton's apartment and shook hands, greeting each of a couple of dozen educators as though he had done nothing else that day and had nothing else to do.

A very serious woman there reminded him that they had

met some years ago on a houseboat in the Vale of Kashmir. "I believe you said it was the nearest to Heaven you'd ever come," the woman said. "I'm so sorry I wasn't here in this country to cast my vote for you."

"And we couldn't spare it," Mr. Stevenson said.

Mr. Stevenson, rushing no one, held a conversation with everybody in the room. Then the educators sat down, and Mr. Stevenson, taking a chair in a corner of the room, started talking to them. Even here, he began by making his listeners laugh. "I don't often get a captive audience," he said, and everything in his expression signified that he was appreciating the fact that he had one now. They laughed. "It's not often that I get the opportunity to talk to such a literate and cultivated audience," he went on. Again they laughed. He added, "There were times, as a Democratic politician, when I never expected that at all." In the next thirty minutes, speaking quickly, he gave a brilliantly clear, concise, and orderly history, description, and explanation of the events leading up to the current difficulty with the back assessments, of Article 19, of the significance of the deadlock, and of the reluctance of any of the countries—even the Soviet Union— to have an out-and-out confrontation with the United States, because they couldn't be sure they would win. Then Mr. Stevenson allowed time for questions. One man asked him if he thought the Russians wanted to break up the U.N., and Mr. Stevenson said no, he thought they would like only to convert the General Assembly into a static debating forum. As he came to a close, he again, irrepressibly, said something to make his listeners laugh: "I remember my father telling me the story of the preacher delivering an exhortation to his flock, and as he reached the climax of his exhortation, a man in the front row got up and said, 'O Lord, use me. Use me, O Lord—in an advisory capacity!' "

As we were leaving Senator Benton's apartment, I asked Mr. Stevenson how in the world he had the strength and the interest, after the day he had put in—a day that was still far from over—to give that much concentrated attention to this small group of workers for UNESCO. His answer had no note of martyrdom in it but was casual and matter-of-fact. He told me, "You don't like to come in and say, 'What the hell, it's useless to try to explain, it's too complicated.' So you try to tell them the score. They should be informed."

The party given for Mr. Stevenson on his sixty fifth birthday was held at the River Club, and was attended by a couple of dozen of his close friends, who had started the tradition of giving him such a party fifteen years earlier in the Executive Mansion in Springfield. During the evening, Mr. Stevenson happened to say that he thought "the fifteenth running of this classic should be the last." He also said, "I've heard that a woman's best years are between thirty-nine and forty. My best years have been the past fifteen. For tomorrow is today, and I shall never be any older than I am now." He had been listening for a couple of hours to funny, nostalgic, and loving remarks about

53

himself, including the reading of "A Composite Portrait of Adlai by His Friends on His Sixty-fifth Birthday," in verse, each stanza having been composed by one of his friends. Mr. Stevenson laughed and cried at his party, and scribbled notes of things he wanted to tell his friends at the end. "The best of one's life is one's friends," he said to them. "I've never thought it necessary to be serious about serious things. It takes only a pin to prick the biggest balloon. Horace Walpole said, 'Old age is no uncomfortable thing if one gives up to it with good grace and doesn't drag it about.' I feel there's so much to do, so much to make up, and I do believe that nothing succeeds like excess. My dearest friends, forgive me my excesses, and I'll forgive you your successes. Give me the benefit of your candor and your criticism, but please keep your doubts to yourself, because I have enough of those of my own."

On the winter morning of the first major air strike in Vietnam, I asked Mr. Stevenson some questions about past Presidents of the United States, and in spite of the crisis of the moment, he replied as though the questions were timely and in order. "I think great Presidents are usually the product of their times," he said at one point. "Abraham Lincoln has always been my hero, as he is the hero of most Americans. As President, he contributed to the world the end of slavery, which was an enormous leap forward in history, but then he was assassinated and he didn't have to live through the Reconstruction and the bitterness that followed the war. No one can say what he might have been had he not been assassinated. Bear in mind, however, that I was raised in Lincoln country. My great-grandfather was Lincoln's friend and the first to propose him for the Presidency. It was to him that Lincoln addressed his autobiography. So I was naturally saturated with Lincoln from infancy. The other figure who is very important to me is Woodrow Wilson. He showed us, on the world scene, an extension of what Lincoln preached; namely, that freedom isn't a limited—a parochial—matter but a universal matter. Also, Wilson was the first President I ever met. When I was a boy of twelve, my father took me to visit President Wilson, then Governor of New Jersey, at his summer house in Sea Girt, New Jersey. It was a hot day in August, 1912, and he was running for President. I mounted the steps of that large frame house alongside my father, and Governor Wilson came out and met us on the porch. He shook hands with me in a formal, courteous way. I was paralyzed with awe. The conversation related mostly to the campaign and how things would go in Illinois. There was a lot of talk about the Democratic Party and the state of mind of people in the Middle West. My father was confident about everything, because of the Bull Moose split. Governor Wilson was extremely courteous to me. He asked me in a friendly, fatherly way if I was interested in politics or in public affairs, and he expressed the hope that I was. You know the way older people often get humble with younger people, and in somewhat that spirit, I think, he made a casual remark about Princeton, and about his having been president of Princeton before becoming Governor of New

Jersey. That's what decided me on going to Princeton, right then and there. I came away with the feeling: I'm his deathless friend. His supporter. His admirer. That's my man." There was affection but no sentimentality in Mr. Stevenson's manner as he talked about Wilson. "And another great President was, of course, Franklin Roosevelt," he went on. "Here, again, there were many contributing factors. The historical ones are obvious. He showed us the way to so many social transformations, bloodlessly. He died in office, from his labors, which always dramatizes and adds an emotional factor to the life of a man."

Mr. Stevenson talked for some time about President Truman, saying he would be entitled to a high mark in history for the way he dealt with the postwar period. Then he went on to talk about John F. Kennedy's extraordinary mind and spirit and promise. "When President Kennedy was assassinated," he said, "we were all left with a sense of incompleteness."

There was one hot, muggy night in the summer of 1964, during the political campaign, when I rode back with Mr. Stevenson on a shuttle plane at the end of one of his incredibly full working days in Washington. It was late when we landed at La Guardia Airport. The city was steaming. Mr. Stevenson was greeted by his driver, who handed him a portfolio of emergency cables and messages to be studied. He did the work in the car as he was riding toward his apartment, and then he remembered that Mayor Wagner had wanted to talk to him about some local aspects of the election campaign, so he asked the driver to stop at Gracie Mansion. It was around ten-thirty when we got there, and we ran into the fading moments of what had been a Young Citizens for Johnson Barbecue, with food prepared by President Johnson's own caterer, imported from Texas. The barbecue seemed to be under the supervision of Lynda Bird Johnson, Robert F. Wagner, Jr., and other very young, very attractive, very recently well-fed Democrats, and they all greeted Mr. Stevenson cordially. It happened that he hadn't had anything to eat since lunch, which he had eaten at the State Department with Dean Rusk. The Gracie Mansion lawn, under festive garden lighting, was strewn with delicious-looking and aromatic-smelling remnants of what had clearly been a great party. Robert Wagner, Jr., said that his father was upstairs, and quickly led Mr. Stevenson up to see the Mayor. Half an hour later, Mr. Stevenson came down. He looked a little hungry but not a bit tired. The party was petering out by then, and the Mayor's guards, who did look tired, were encouraging the young guests to leave. Everybody assumed—wrongly, I thought—that Mr. Stevenson wanted to get away as fast as possible.

Mr. Stevenson seemed to be peering wistfully at the Gracie Mansion lawn. It looked inviting, that hot, humid, misty night, with paper picnic plates dotted about, and with suntanned, laughing young men and women standing around in clusters, talking, presumably, about the campaign, and with President Johnson's caterer—fat and jolly, wrapped in a huge white apron, and wearing a chef's tall white hat—still overseeing a long table laden with steaks, sweet corn, and spareribs. But the party was technically over, and a solicitous guard was ushering Mr. Stevenson out to his car. He went. The guard saluted and left him. Mr. Stevenson's driver opened the car door. Just then, a young couple, both tall and skinny and both wearing sandals and blue jeans, the girl with long blond hair falling loosely over the collar of a shirtwaist blouse and the boy with a cultivated fringe of beard, strolled over to Mr. Stevenson, holding hands. They smiled at him and coolly asked him what was going on at Gracie Mansion. A party, he told them. They looked happy and lazy and not impressed, and strolled away, still holding hands. Mr. Stevenson stood there a moment or two, looking down the street after them, and as he got into his car he said, "Summer in New York is pretty wonderful, isn't it?"

PHOTO CREDITS